Read-About® Health

Grains

By Carol Alexander

Consultants
Reading Adviser
Nanci R. Vargus, EdD
Assistant Professor of Literacy
University of Indianapolis, Indianapolis, Indiana

Subject Adviser
Janet M. Gilchrist, PhD, RD
Nutritionist

Children's Press®
A Division of Scholastic Inc.
New York   Toronto   London   Auckland   Sydney
Mexico City   New Delhi   Hong Kong
Danbury, Connecticut

Designer: Herman Adler Design
Photo Researcher: Caroline Anderson
The photo on the cover shows different sources of grains.

Library of Congress Cataloging-in-Publication Data

Alexander, Carol, 1955–
  Grains / by Carol Alexander.
    p. cm. — (Rookie read-about health)
  Includes index.
  ISBN 0-516-23646-6 (lib. bdg.)   0-516-24649-6 (pbk.)
  1. Cereals as food—Juvenile literature. 2. Grain—Juvenile literature. I. Title.
II. Series.
  TX393.A44 2005
  641.3'31—dc22   2005004777

1 2 3 4 5 6 7 8 9 10 R 14 13 12 11 10 09 08 07 06 05

Did you know that your body needs fuel?

Food is the body's fuel.
It gives us the energy to
work and play.

Grains are power foods.
Some examples of grains
are brown rice, oats,
wheat, and corn.

These grains are used to
make bread, pasta, cereals,
and other foods.

8

Grains come from plants
called cereal grasses.

A whole grain includes
every part of a plant
that can be eaten.
Whole grains have
carbohydrates, fiber,
vitamins, and minerals.

These are nutrients.
You need nutrients to
stay healthy.

Grains are complex carbohydrates. They are high-energy foods.

Complex carbohydrates quickly break down into glucose, a simple sugar.

Glucose is stored in our muscles as something called glycogen.

When we exercise, glycogen turns into quick energy.

People all over the world eat grains. Most of the world's food energy supply comes from grains.

The rest comes from vegetables, fruits, meats, fish, nuts, eggs, and dairy foods.

15

Farmers in the United States grow many different grain crops. Corn and wheat are just a few examples.

The United States sells some of its grain to other countries.

First, farmers gather the grain crop.

Next, the grain is ground up, or milled. The milled grain is kept cool and dry in special sacks.

19

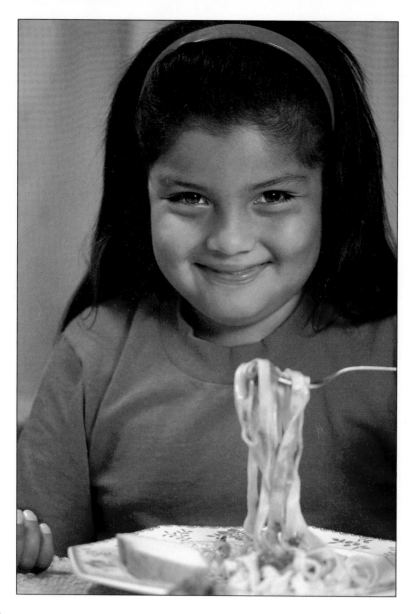

Grain is sometimes ground into flour.

Flour is used to make bread, pasta, and other foods. Whole wheat flour is best for you.

Scientists came up with the Food Guidance System. It tells you how many times a day you should eat different foods to stay healthy.

MyPyramid.gov
STEPS TO A HEALTHIER YOU

Grain Group
Make half your grains whole

Vegetable Group
Vary your veggies

Fruit Group
Focus on fruits

Milk Group
Get your calcium-rich foods

Meat & Bean Group
Go lean with protein

Try to eat at least three servings of whole grains each day.

Whole grain cereals, breads, and crackers are good choices.

Brown rice, popcorn, and rice cakes are some other examples of whole grains.

You can find many kinds of bread and grains at grocery stores. These foods are tasty and filling.

It's easy to be a power eater!

Words You Know

bread

cereal

crackers

exercise

grains

pasta

popcorn

rice

Index

About the Author

Carol Alexander has written both fiction and nonfiction for children and young adults. She has taught English in colleges around the New York City area. She lives in Manhattan with her husband and daughter.

Photo Credits

Photographs © 2005: Corbis Images: 3 (Roy Morsch), 7 center, 15, 31 bottom right, 31 top right (Royalty-Free); Envision Stock Photography Inc.: 25 top right, 30 bottom left (Mark Ferri), 25 bottom right (MAK Studio), 6, 7 bottom, 30 top (Madeline Polss), 25 top left; Omni-Photo Communications: 19 (Anthony Blake), 8, 16 (Fotopic); Peter Arnold Inc./Jodi Jacobson: cover; PhotoEdit: 12, 31 top left (Myrleen Ferguson Cate), 29 (Tom McCarthy), 20 (David Young-Wolff); PictureQuest/Brand X Pictures/Benjamin F. Fink Jr.: 25 bottom left, 31 bottom left; Randy Matusow: 5, 11, 26, 30 bottom right.